Living without You

A Guide on How to Live after
the Loss of your Loved One.

By Pastor Barbra Sonnen-Hernandez, LMFT

Living without You©2022

Written by Barbra Sonnen-Hernandez

Edited by Ella Massaquoi

Copyright©2022 Barbra Sonnen-Hernandez

All rights reserved.

ISBN:9798849743769

CONTENTS

CHAPTER ONE: ACCEPTING DEATH

Losing a loved one can be very traumatic. Emotions can come from all kinds of directions. Some of these emotions you didn't even know you had. Others may have been building up for a time. Regardless, it becomes an encounter with another kind of life.

Unexpected death of a loved one, such as an accident or sudden health scare, is extremely difficult. There were no goodbyes or time to spend the last days together. Emotions in these circumstances can turn to anger, blaming others for the death even if no one was truly at fault. Over all, it comes down to feeling such sorrow for the loss of the loved one.

Some death occurrences can be accepted peacefully. This may be when loved ones die of old age or a long-term illness. You were aware that death would occur, and by making the arrangements and taking care of personal items for your loved one, you could prepare for their death. This may have relieved you of sorrow for the time spent and the help you did for your loved one because they were not alone. It can make you feel as if the both of you are going through the death process together. After your loved one's death, you might realize that your life has now been fulfilled by knowing the reality of death. So now your life begins with a much better understanding of the meaning of death.

Whether the death was unexpected or you were prepared for it, losing a loved one can begin a new journey that is always unexpected no matter what amount of time you had with your loved one.

As a Pastor, I have officiated at many funerals and counseled many families undergoing the sorrow of losing their loved one. I've learned that not every case is the same. In gathering all my resources, case by case, this handbook is to help guide you step by step on how to manage all kinds of emotions associated with loss and how to live without your loved one.

CHAPTER TWO:
THE DAYS AFTER DEATH

The very day that your loved one has died, a state of shock in the body, mind and spirit occurs. Your body becomes very tired, and you might pull away from your family, friends and surroundings. Everything is distant and nothing seems to matter. All energy has been sucked out of you, and your appetite for food has deteriorated. This process can take days or even weeks. Be aware that if it does continue to go on for several weeks or months, you might be going through depression. This is a normal process and counseling would be the best method to get treated. You don't want to let this linger on.

Lots of crying and sleepless nights are also very typical of losing a loved one. The following day where you don't hear, see or talk with your loved one can bring on much sadness since the realization of never being with your loved one becomes a fear episode. You start to experience loneliness and helplessness.

Many questions start to enter your mind such as "Who is going to fix this?", "What will I do with their possessions?" "How can I take care of the children?" A huge amount of stress falls upon you.

As you undergo this process, you are thinking as two. Your mind has no concept of taking these matters into your own hands and making the decisions on your own. You relied so much on the person who is gone that without them this becomes a new life with many challenges.

Throughout this whirlwind of emotions, you may have to stay on course to complete the death process by making the funeral arrangements and taking care of the finances. Getting a family member or friend to help make phone calls to inform those who need to know of the death of your loved one can be a big help. Many people want to give their condolences and want to comfort you. This is a good time to let someone else inform the family to give you space to reflect on this great loss. When it seems time to talk, then you should reach out to those concerned about you. Talking with those who knew your loved one and who were very close to them, helps the healing process for the both of you.

Give yourself time during these next days to deal with one thing at a time. The main focus right now is to tend to the funeral arrangements and to make sure your loved one gets to their final resting place. Just don't try to do everything yourself or in one day. Each day is hard enough to deal with. The funeral home can help you with all the arrangements, and they'll do it with much dignity and care since they understand what you are going through.

Staying focused, staying strong and a little bit of praying will help ease the stress and loneliness during the days ahead.

***

I remember working with a family that lost their mother. The father was already deceased. Even though the mother had a long-term illness, it still was a lot for the family. They felt alone now that the mother was gone. Making funeral decisions on their own made them uneasy and stressed. They wanted everything perfect for her funeral, but they still didn't feel if that's what their mother wanted.

As I spoke with the family, I told them that this was a normal feeling. It meant that they loved their mother so much that they wanted the best for her funeral because she gave them all the best from her. I encouraged them to let go of that stress and trust that they were doing the right thing. She lived her whole life serving not only as a mother and wife, but with a spirit of love that will continue to shine through her family.

Talking with them made such a big difference in how they viewed the process of grief and losing a loved one. It is my hope you are beginning to feel the same.

CHAPTER THREE: EMOTIONS

By the second and third week, your body starts to function again. The loss of your loved one is still there—tears haven't gone away—but this time it comes in episodes. Hunger starts to come back in force, and you find yourself eating more than you should. This is a time to watch this process of eating. Yes, food gives us energy, but we also need to be aware of the types of food to eat during this time and how much. Depression can make food seem like your friend and result in being over-weight.

That is another change in your life you don't need. The focus at this time is to eat healthy, so going to your doctor to get nutritional guidance would be the right course. Get out and exercise. Taking care of your health will give you the motivation to think more clearly on what you need to take care of at home, work and with family and friends.

Once you begin getting stronger and

have accepted that your loved one is gone from your sight, the body begins to awaken past memories and unfinished business with your loved one. This might be where you start to get angry, moody and unhappy. In some cases, unfinished business could mean an affair found out, an abuse remembered, an alcoholic, or drug addiction or even realization of a loveless marriage. Our mind has a tendency to draw attention to these offenses that were stored inside of you, and once the loved one has passed away, everything boils up. You want so much to bring your loved one back to stand trial for what they have placed on you.

Even the perfect loved one who took care of you, was always there for you, and loved you unconditionally, can result in anger against them for not being there anymore to give you that love again. You know you are at it alone, and the love given now from your own family and friends is not the same. Everything including hugs and kisses, laughter and talks are very different now.

All these emotions are normal when losing a loved one. It's not strange or unusual. It's your life trying to discover a new journey—a journey into life without your loved one.

***

I kept in touch with a woman who lost her husband to terminal cancer. She had her husband cremated but never made the time to scatter his ashes at a favorite spot he loved. Instead, she kept the urn on top of her fireplace mantel in her living room. She told me jokingly that whenever she would remember a bad memory with him, she would go up to the urn and scold him. I'd ask her how frequently she would do this, and she mentioned it was several times a week.

I then asked her if she was still planning on scattering his ashes. She looked thoughtfully at me and said it would be a good idea to finally put him to rest. We planned the date, and I went with her to the favorite spot her husband loved. She cried so much as if he just died. This was a big step for her, and even though her husband had already passed away, this moment marked the true beginning of her life without him.

CHAPTER FOUR: FORGIVENESS

In order for you to move on into your new life, you have to learn to forgive your loved one. This will take time as you enter into different emotions. Whatever circumstances you might have had in your relationship with your loved one, there was probably something that caused a conflict, misunderstanding or argument. Yet, forgiveness is about letting go.

When you dwell on things of the past that made you angry or upset with your loved one, you will tend to hang on to that memory so that the death process will make you less sorrowful. This is not a good habit to start. A healthy way to release the hurt and sorrow you are undergoing is through crying, talking about how you feel, and what you are going through. This is a natural way to process and allow the body to release the stress and anxieties of this traumatic experience in your life.

Holding on to the anger of your loved one won't bring them back. It only adds another stressful thing to deal with.

When you forgive, let go of everything. That's not to say you will forget the beautiful memories you once shared with your loved one—by no means, you never want to forget those memories since they bring closure and strengthen you to realize you are on your own now. With time, you can also begin to learn from the good memories that might help guide you in your life.

When you don't forgive by not letting go, it can become very difficult when you think of a memory. You tend to put aside happy memories and look for a reason that caused you to be angry. This then leads to holding back the tears and sorrow of your loss, making it seem like you're doing just fine when you're not.

Keep in mind that forgiveness is a type of love leading to a closure. It's an end to what started wrong, making it right. So, if you don't want to deal with forgiveness of your loved one, it might remain wrong for quite awhile, and it could cause other troubling situations for a future relationship.

To begin your new life without your loved one, forgiveness is the start. If you're having difficulty with this, seeing a professional spiritual counselor can help.

***

Three sisters lost their beloved mother due to several health complications. The eldest sister was the one who took care of the mother day and night. During the funeral service, the other two younger sisters were happy talking about precious memories with their mother while the oldest was filled with anger and bitterness towards the other sisters for going about as they were.

When it came time for the burial, I approached the oldest sister privately and told her that her work in taking care of her mother day and night was not forgotten and that her mother really appreciated what she did. The daughter cried hearing these words. Sometimes in our own distress we forget to touch base with those around us who really need the words and sincerity. Without it, the attitude can result in a longtime bitterness even in their own lives.

.

CHAPTER FIVE: TIME TO HEAL

A funeral service can bring on the same emotions as when the death occurred, but it can also give you time to reflect on your loved one. As you have already started your life alone, the funeral service is a time of respect for your loved one to be at rest and at peace. Crying begins again, and this time not so much for the loss, but for the fond memories the two of you shared.

By now, you made it through the funeral service and a few weeks have gone by. At this time, you have been living on your own and making your own decisions. You're eating and sleeping again. You might have noticed that your sleeping pattern has changed. You seem to be up more at night due to fear and being alone. This tendency takes time to break until you become stronger and more confident in yourself taking the lead now.

Getting out, walking and breathing fresh air not only helps with your physical body, but your spiritual one as well. Accomplishing tasks and focusing on priorities in your new life is the direction you should go. It's okay to get some help from time to time from loved ones and caring friends. Remember they too are at a loss and this is their way to help the both of you heal.

***

At the funeral service I was officiating at, a man had lost his beloved wife suddenly. He was in a wheelchair and his adult son by his side had a disability as well. When I approached the gentleman and gave my condolences, he angrily asked me if I was truly sorry for his loss. As I began to quote some scripture to him in the hopes of calming him down a bit, he interrupted me in questioning why God would take her away from him. I explained to him that we do not know the hour or day God takes us from this earth.

He then asked, who will take care of me? She was always there for me and when I became gravely ill, she never left my side. I told him that she has been gone for 2 weeks now and then asked who has been taking care of him? He said he manages but it's been hard not having her there in case he needed her. I told him how proud I was to hear that he has really tried to do things alone and that it was a natural feeling for him to miss her. She was his rock and his strength and that's something as her example she left for him to now give to his son so that between the two of them they can be strong in the life ahead without her.

As he cried immensely, I hugged him and let him know what a blessing his wife was to him. If we see more of the blessings of our loved ones and the wonderful relationship you had with them, then it makes the memories a happy one. It's during those times that we can connect with their spirit to encourage your spirit to begin your new memories in your single life.

CHAPTER SIX: A NEW LIFE

Throughout the weeks, months and even years, your loved one is never forgotten. You will always feel them in spirit whether it's through a memory or a sign of something unexpected happening. They will always be with you through love they gave to you, you gave to them, and now, give to others.

It's time to make new memories, new families, new friends and to embrace what death means. It's a process we will all undertake someday. Since you experienced it, you may be able to help others who are dealing with grief for the first time. It will make you a better and stronger person living alone and making life's decisions alone. If you choose to live with a family member and sell everything you had with your loved one, this is a normal process and is common with elderly people. It's good to live with another loved one who will take care of you in ways you cannot help yourself.

The family support system is always a

good idea if you have that. They are people you can depend on to help at home or to enjoy visiting with. If you don't have that, making new friends through your local church or community will get you started in enjoying things you never did before or didn't have the time to.

Start enjoying your life. Go on walks, take a friend for lunch, adopt a pet, travel and see the world! Remember that Death is not the end but a Victory! Your loved one is now on a new journey. It's time to enjoy your new journey without them on earth. Make new memories and enjoy every minute of your life.

***

A single mother who lost her child at childbirth seemed so distant and melancholy from the time of the birth to the funeral service. She was a very young girl whose pregnancy was unexpected. The adoptive parents of the baby were in attendance at the funeral service with a very small gathering. As I approached the baby's natural mother, being very concerned for her well-being, she told me how sad she was for the adoptive parents. They had been with her since she was pregnant and took good care of all her needs. She didn't have any words to say at the service because she told me the grief was so overwhelming to see.

In turn, I told her how strong and compassionate she was for the couple. But, I needed to ask her how she felt about losing the baby. She answered eloquently and said the baby is now well taken care of and has a huge family in heaven watching over. She continued saying that it's her turn to take care of the couple in their loss and be there for them as they were for her.

I was amazed how much she had matured, not only as a mother to be but in how much she understood that having friends and family to help her cope with this loss is just as much for others.

MEDITATION

The Following are Quotes and Scriptures to inspire and strengthen you while you are going through your new life without your loved one.

When a loved one dies, it is natural for us to feel a sense of loss and even a deep loneliness. That will not vanish overnight. But even when we feel the pain of bereavement most intensely, we can also know the gracious and loving presence of Christ most closely.

-Billy Graham

"In every disappointment, great or small. Let your heart fly directly to your dear Savior, throwing yourself in those arms for refuge against every pain and sorrow. Jesus will never leave you or forsake you."

-Elizabeth Ann Seton

In Our Hearts

We thought of you today.
But that is nothing new.
We thought about you yesterday.
And days before that too.
We think of you in silence.
We often speak your name.
Now all we have are memories.
And your picture in a frame.
Your memory is our keepsake.
With which we'll never part.
God has you in his keeping.
We have you in our heart.

-Unknown

"There is a sacredness in tears. They are not the mark of weakness, but of power. They speak more eloquently than ten thousand tongues. They are the messengers of overwhelming grief, of deep contrition, and of unspeakable love."

-Washington Irving

"The Lord is near to the brokenhearted and saves the crushed in spirit."

Psalm 34:18

"Blessed are those who mourn, for they shall be comforted."

-Matthew 5:4

"Say not in grief 'he is no more' but live in thankfulness that he was."

-Hebrew proverb

"We need never be afraid of our tears."

-Charles Dickens

SUMMARY

Chp. 1: ACCEPTING DEATH

Emotions
Understanding the type of death

Chp. 2: THE DAYS AFTER DEATH

Distant from people
Low energy
No appetite
Depression
Crying
Sleeplessness
Fear
Loneliness
Helplessness
Stress

Chp. 3: EMOTIONS

Episodes of crying come and go
Increase of Appetite
Healthy eating
Exercise
Angry
Moody

Unhappy
Offended
Loneliness

Chp. 4: FORGIVENESS

Letting go
Crying
Closure
Strength
Love
Professional Spiritual Counseling

Chp. 5: TIME TO HEAL

Living independently
Normal appetite
Change of sleeping pattern
Fear continues
Continue exercising
Put priorities in order
Get help at times

Chp. 6: A NEW LIFE

Never forgetting your loved one
New memories
Meaning of Death

Help others with a loved one's loss
Living independently or with family
Family support
Making new friends
Join local church or community
Take walks
Enjoy lunch with a friend
Adopt a pet
Travel
Enjoy your new life

ABOUT THE AUTHOR

Pastor Barbra Sonnen-Hernandez is a Licensed Marriage and Family Therapist and has written several inspirational and motivational books to encourage others in life's journeys. She has spoken at many events in order to spread the word of faith and hope. As a pastoral counselor, she felt this handbook was needed to help so many people dealing with loss and grief—a part of her life she knows very well.
You can visit her Ministry at:
www.barbrasonnenhernandez.com

NOTES

Made in the USA
Columbia, SC
30 June 2023